Jazz Book

10 Original Piano Solos
With Optional CD Accompaniments

Mike Springer

"I want to play another jazz piece!" Many teachers have heard this sentiment voiced in their studios—and for good reason. Jazz is fun to play!

Not Just Another Jazz Book is the third addition to the growing "Not Just Another" series. Beginning with *Not Just Another Scale Book,* three books that hide scales within pieces in all keys, the series continued with *Not Just Another Christmas Book,* three books that feature jazzy arrangements of classic Christmas tunes. Included in *Not Just Another Jazz Book* are original compositions that feature swing, blues, ragtime, and Latin styles.

Additionally, all the books are truly unique because they contain innovative and fun orchestrated background tracks for each solo. Each piece has three different CD tracks in the following order:

- For listening, the *Performance Model Track* features the piano, bass, and drums in a complete performance.

- For practicing, the *Practice Tempo Track* features the bass and drums (without the piano solo) at a slower tempo.

- For performing, the *Performance Tempo Track* features the bass and drums (without the piano solo) at the performance tempo.

For practice and performance ease, a two-measure drum lead-in is given at the beginning of every CD track. Metronome markings for both tempos are given at the beginning of each arrangement.

Get ready to jam out and have some fun with *Not Just Another Jazz Book,* Book 2!

Contents

in honor of Perrin Holder

Alfred Music
P.O. Box 10003
Van Nuys, CA 91410-0003
alfred.com

Copyright © 2013 by Alfred Music
All rights reserved. Produced in USA.

No part of this book shall be reproduced, arranged, adapted, recorded, publicly performed, stored in a retrieval system, or transmitted by any means without written permission from the publisher. In order to comply with copyright laws, please apply for such written permission and/or license by contacting the publisher at alfred.com/permissions.

ISBN-10: 0-7390-9370-3
ISBN-13: 978-0-7390-9370-2

Cover Photos
Abstract music red background: © shutterstock.com / lem • Stand up bass Vector: © shutterstock.com / KET-SMM • Drum kit isolated on a white background: © shutterstock.com / lem

Red River Rag

1 Performance Model
2 Practice Tempo (♩ = 132)
3 Performance Tempo (♩ = 184)

Mike Springer

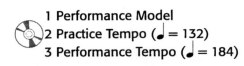

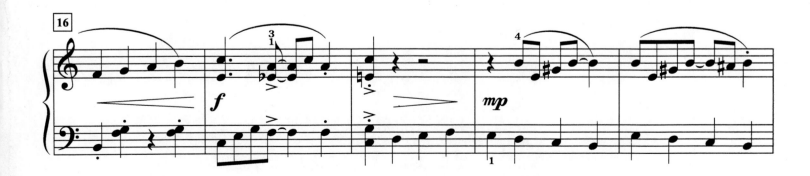

Monday Morning Blues

4 Performance Model
5 Practice Tempo (♩ = 63)
6 Performance Tempo (♩ = 84)

Mike Springer

Big Band Jam

7 Performance Model
8 Practice Tempo (♩ = 92)
9 Performance Tempo (♩ = 120)

Mike Springer

Memories of You

10 Performance Model
11 Practice Tempo (♩ = 63)
12 Performance Tempo (♩ = 88)

Mike Springer

Summer Break!

13 Performance Model
14 Practice Tempo (♩ = 120)
15 Performance Tempo (♩ = 168)

Mike Springer

Walkin' Down the Avenue

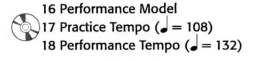

16 Performance Model
17 Practice Tempo (♩ = 108)
18 Performance Tempo (♩ = 132)

Mike Springer

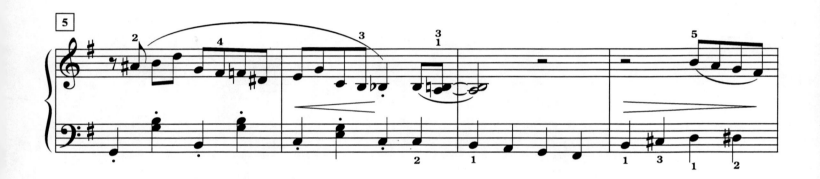

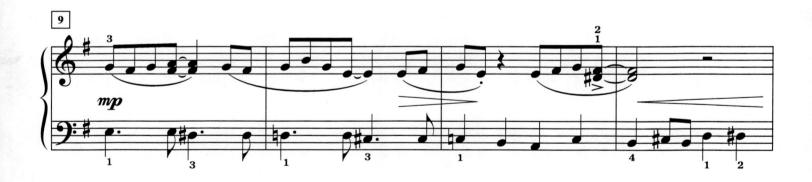

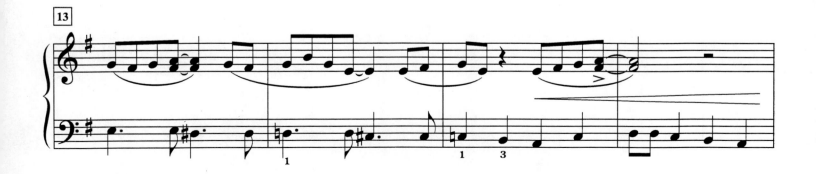

Sunset in Rio

19 Performance Model
20 Practice Tempo (♩ = 120)
21 Performance Tempo (♩ = 176)

Mike Springer

Keepin' Cool

22 Performance Model
23 Practice Tempo (♩ = 92)
24 Performance Tempo (♩ = 120)

Mike Springer

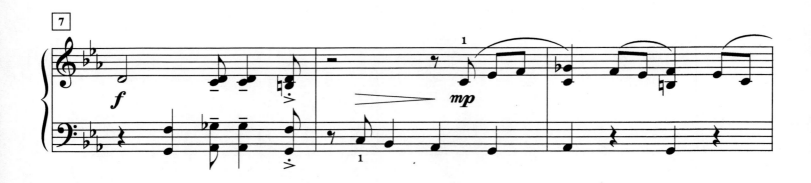

Rebel Rock!

25 Performance Model
26 Practice Tempo (♩ = 96)
27 Performance Tempo (♩ = 144)

Mike Springer

London Lights

28 Performance Model
29 Practice Tempo ($\quad$ = 92)
30 Performance Tempo ($\quad$ = 132)

Mike Springer